J.
21
Wil

Laura Ingalls Wilder

By Pamela Walker

Children's Press
A Division of Scholastic Inc.
New York / Toronto / London / Auckland / Sydney
Mexico City / New Delhi / Hong Kong
Danbury, Connecticut

Photo Credits: Cover and pp. 5, 9, 11, 15, 17, 21 Laura Ingalls Wilder Museum, Mansfield, MO; pp. 7,13 © Corbis; p. 19 photo by Cindy Reiman; pp. 5, 11, 15 © Image Farm (The Antique Frame Collection)
Contributing Editor: Jennifer Silate
Book Design: Victoria Johnson

Visit Children's Press on the Internet at:
http://publishing.grolier.com

Library of Congress Cataloging-in-Publication Data

Walker, Pamela, 1958-
 Laura Ingalls Wilder / by Pamela Walker.
     p. cm. -- (Real people)
   Includes index.
   ISBN 0-516-23435-8 (lib. bdg.) -- ISBN 0-516-23589-3 (pbk.)
   1. Wilder, Laura Ingalls, 1867-1957--Juvenile literature. 2. Authors, American--20th century--Biography--Juvenile literature. 3. Frontier and pioneer life--United States--Juvenile literature. 4. Children's stories--Authorship--Juvenile literature. [1. Wilder, Laura Ingalls, 1867-1957. 2. Authors, American. 3. Women--Biography. 4. Frontier and pioneer life.] I. Title.

 PS3545.I342 Z927 2001
 813'.52--dc21
[B]
                                                              2001017270

Contents

Meet Laura Ingalls Wilder.

5

Laura lived in a **log cabin** with her family.

Laura had a big family.

She had three sisters.

Laura was very close with her sisters.

11

Laura liked to read.

She liked school.

Laura became a teacher.

EAU CLAIRE DISTRICT LIBRA

13

Laura married Almanzo Wilder.

They had a daughter named Rose.

15

This was Laura's desk.

She sat at this desk and wrote **stories** about her life.

The stories are called the Little House books.

Children still read her books today.

Many people like Laura's books.

She is a very **famous** writer.

21

New Words

famous (**fay**-muhs) very well known

log cabin (**lawg cab**-uhn) a small house
   made with trees

stories (**stor**-eez) tales about an event

To Find Out More

Books
Going West
by Laura Ingalls Wilder
HarperCollins Children's Books

Laura Ingalls Wilder: An Author's Story
by Sarah Glassock
Raintree Steck-Vaughn Publishers

Web Site
Little House Home
http://www.littlehousebooks.com/
This Web site has information about Laura Ingalls Wilder's life. It also has recipes and activities from pioneer times.

Index

About the Author
Pamela Walker was born in Kentucky. When she grew up, she moved to New York and became a writer.

Reading Consultants
Kris Flynn, Coordinator, Small School District Literacy, The San Diego County Office of Education

Shelly Forys, Certified Reading Recovery Specialist, W.J. Zahnow Elementary School, Waterloo, IL

Sue McAdams, Former President of the North Texas Reading Council of the IRA, and Early Literary Consultant, Dallas, TX